M000036519

It's Okay to Take a

NAP

and

Other Reassuring Truths for
MOTHERS EVERYWHERE

Contents

Acknowledgments

With deepest admiration and appreciation:

To everyone at Cedar Fort, Inc.: Kammi Rencher for suggesting I write this book; Annaliese Cox for her editing expertise; Melanee Dahl and Angie Harris for the enormous good they do in book promotion; Lyle Mortimer for his belief in me as an author; and everyone else at Cedar Fort who had a hand in bringing this book to life.

To Alexandra Stoddard, author extraordinaire: I will never forget the day I happened across your book *Living a Beautiful Life* in a Houston bookstore some twenty years ago. I have anxiously awaited the publication of each of your books since (your twenty-sixth book is due out as I write this). Thank you for your thoughtful mentoring of me and so many others. Inspired by your example, I seek to choose happiness every day.

To my mom and dad, Bill and Joyce Sansing: You are exactly the right parents for me. Thanks for having me. Thanks for raising me with a strong work ethic and the sense that I can make a difference in the world. And, most of all, thanks for loving me all of my life. I can't help but love you too.

To my sisters, Lea Giberson, Mary Ellsworth, and Rebecca Adling: Oh how I wish we lived closer to each other. Perhaps someday we will. Until then, let's continue to share our journey through motherhood and family life the best we can. I love you.

To my dear husband, Barry: I wish everyone could know the happiness I have known with you. We have certainly faced our share of tough times over the years, but there is no one I would rather face those times with than you. Thank you for being there for me. I love you and will be there for you forever.

To my beloved children, Amanda, Samantha, Kelly, Charlotte, and Brady: I could fill a book with all the reasons I love being your mom. Thanks for being my children. You never cease to amaze me. You are each so different and yet each so completely lovable. What an amazing adventure together we've had so far. Never forget my favorite question of you: *Who loves you?* And your sure answer: *Mama loves me.* Yes, that's right; I love you, always and forever.

Being a One-of-a-Kind Mom Is the Best

1

If we as mothers do something we absolutely love alongside raising children we absolutely love, we will, I believe, almost guarantee that our children will be raised in an atmosphere steeped in joy.

Can you imagine what the world would be like if all the mothers in the world were exactly alike in how they behaved, in their approach to motherhood, and in the strengths and talents they shared with their families? I confess I feel great relief in knowing that we can each be our own kind of mom, a complete original, unlike any other mother on the face of the planet.

My mom was certainly one of a kind. Like most mothers, she sought to feed, clothe, and shelter us well and to educate and raise us to be responsible adults. But one of the things that set her apart from all the other mothers I knew was her talent for sewing and clothing design. She didn't make herself do these things. She loved doing them, and so she wove them quite naturally into the fabric of motherhood and family life.

She always had a project in progress—whether it was Easter dresses or play clothes for my three sisters and me. I never had to worry about wearing the same outfit as another little girl because my mom's creations were each completely unique and made with just me in mind.

Because my mother loved sewing, the significant moments in my life can be recalled, to a great extent, with the dresses she has made for me over the years. There were the powder blue Easter dresses for starters (powder blue, she felt certain, was my color). But there were also the royal blue Swiss-dot gown trimmed in cream I wore to my first holiday ball, the pearly mauve southern belle dress she custom-designed for my senior prom, and, of course, the simple but exquisitely bustled white cotton wedding dress she created for my wedding.

When I think of all the beautiful clothes my mother created for my sisters and me, I feel the tiniest twinge of regret that I haven't spent more time sewing for my own children. My mother taught and encouraged me to sew, and while I enjoyed sewing as a teen and felt satisfied with the outfits I made, sewing hasn't been one of my top priorities in my adult years.

As a woman and a mother, I find myself drawn most powerfully to a love of language, reading, and writing, and I enjoy sharing these loves with my children. I definitely agree with the phrase "so many books and so little time." Even so, I try to make the most of the time I have with my kids by sharing the books I love. I find great delight in rediscovering and sharing with my children some of the books I enjoyed as a child; among them—*Go, Dog. Go!* by P. D. Eastman, William Steig's *Sylvester and the Magic Pebble*, as well as chapter books like *The Twenty-One Balloons* by Pene William du Bois and *The Secret Garden* by Frances Hodgson Burnett. And my children and I have enjoyed discovering some new and wonderful books together. We have become especially fond of *Snuggle Puppy* by Sandra Boynton and *Walter: The Story of a Rat* by Barbara Wersba.

Just as a good portion of my childhood can be reconstructed by looking back at the dresses my mother made for me, my children's childhoods are, in large part, being constructed with the books we read and love together. Inspired by the stories we've shared, my children have, in their own imaginative play, lived as boxcar children, explored their own secret gardens, and survived the Dust Bowl of the 1930s.

Given the beautiful clothes my mom has made (for her children and grandchildren) and the love of literature I have shared in my home, I think my children realize that it is not only possible but preferable that a mother pursue a great love—whether that love be sewing or reading and writing or sports or something else—while raising children she loves. If we as mothers do something we absolutely love alongside raising children we absolutely love, we will, I believe, almost guarantee that our children will be raised in an atmosphere steeped in joy.

As I write this, it is clear to me that our children need not share our same interests to the extent we feel them, but that by seeing us pursue and develop our particular hobbies and talents, they will receive the permission they need to discover and nurture their own great hobbies and talents.

The dresses my mother sewed were, for me, the intersection of her love for sewing and her love for me. I love the written word—reading it and writing it. Thus the books in our home and the stories I've shared with my children are the intersection of my love for the written word and my love for them.

As I think about this, I cannot help but contemplate what intersections of love might occur in my children's lives when they someday become parents themselves. My oldest daughter, now seventeen years old and four years older than my next child, is very likely to be the first of my children to have children of her own.

To a great extent, she shares my love of reading and writing and my mother's love of creating things with her hands (she draws and paints beautifully). In particular, she loves to write and illustrate children's picture books. But when I think of what this daughter might someday be like as a mother, I imagine the thing that will set her apart and make her a mother like no other is her love of fun and her penchant for being a ham. She has long possessed the gift of an almost unbounded sense of humor. Unlike me, nothing embarrasses her. She's prone to impromptu slapstick comedy routines that leave the rest of us with bellyaches from laughing. I've told her more than once that she's part Lucille Ball and part Carol Burnett with a sprinkling of Drew Barrymore thrown in. And while she may, in some respects, remind me of these three women, she leaves me with no doubt that she is very much her own woman and will, most assuredly, be her own kind of mom. It is clear to me even now that there will be no shortage of fun and laughter in her home.

This same daughter, when she was about eight years old, wrote a picture book for me called *Moms*. She illustrated it in her vibrant and boldly colored signature style, filling it with pictures of moms in all sizes, shapes, colors, and styles. Her short but sweet story reads, "Some moms are big; some moms are small. Some moms are short; some moms are tall. Some moms are cool; some moms are quiet. Some moms are black, some moms are white, but my mom is just right [meaning, of course, just right for me]."

All these years later, my daughter's story reminds me that we moms need not be exactly alike, that each mother can have her special way of being in the world, of being with her children. And, if we will act on these truths, we can give ourselves the permission we need to use our unique gifts and talents to be our own kind of moms, the kind of moms who are themselves, and in being themselves, just right for the children in their care.

Invitations & Inspirations

"The most important thing she'd learned over the years was that there was no way to be a perfect mother and a million ways to be a good one," says Jill Churchill in *Grime and Punishment.*[1]

❀ Invite your children to share your interests, whatever they may be—sewing, baking, sports, or something entirely different—but be sure to give them the space they need to discover their own. It is a wondrous thing to watch a child discover what he loves and then make it a regular part of his life.

❀ When you see or hear a mother bemoan the fact that she doesn't have such-and-such talent like so-and-so has, remind her of the gifts and talents she does possess that truly bless her family.

❀ Make a list of some of the activities you enjoyed doing as a child—perhaps bicycling, creating collages, or playing softball—and see if you can make room for one or more of them in your life now. It really is possible to do things you love while raising kids you love.

❀ Check out *You Can Do It: The Merit Badge Handbook for Grown-Up Girls* by Lauren Catuzzi Grandcolas (with Yvette Bozzini) for some serious inspiration in creating a life you love by doing things you love on your own and with your children.

❀ Remember, your children are watching. By being yourself and doing things you love, you will show your children how to be themselves and do things they love. And everyone will be the happier for it.

Notes

1. Rosalie Maggio, ed., *The New Beacon Book of Quotations by Women* (Boston: Beacon Press, 1996), 458.

I want better for my children than a mother who exhausts herself
with her perpetual race to the end of a never-ending to-do list.

If I asked you to make a complete to-do list, meaning a to-do list of everything—absolutely everything—you would like to get done in the next few weeks with your children, for your children, in your home and yard, and away from home, how long do you think your list would be? My guess is that it would end up so long you'd have to take a nap halfway through writing it to regain the energy, strength, and, yes, courage necessary to return and complete it.

And then, if you're like me, once you finished writing your to-do list and saw in black and white exactly what you expect of yourself on a regular basis, you'd likely want to crumple the to-do list into the tiniest ball possible and pitch it into the garbage can. You'd realize that no human being could ever accomplish everything on such a list, even if given a lifetime, so why even try?

I can't speak for all moms about why we so often expect more of ourselves than we can possibly deliver, but it seems to me that most of us are, at least to some extent, vulnerable to the media pressure to live up to a false but glorious ideal of motherhood. I am a confident mother, blazing my own trail through motherhood and family life, but even so, I sometimes feel I don't measure up as mother, household manager, and citizen when I read or see the profiles and stories of some of the more prominent and astonishingly productive mothers featured in the press. Namely, I find myself feeling a little inadequate when I see stories about certain celebrity mothers who seem to do it all—and I mean do it all—with astonishing energy and pizzazz.

There's one celebrity mother in particular who has been heavily and favorably featured in the press in recent years. She loves being a mother and makes it clear in interviews that being a mom is indeed her number one priority. And while being a mom is her top priority, raising her children is only the beginning of her hands-on endeavors. She also happens to be a hardworking actress, a Hollywood star (being an actress and a star are, in my estimation, two entirely different jobs), a devoted partner, a world traveler, a high-profile champion of important charitable and social causes, and, yes, let's not forget, the owner of an immaculate and beautifully decorated home worthy of a spread in any glossy magazine.

When I see this mother's life and stack mine against

hers, I can't help but ask, "How does she do it?" And in an attempt to answer this question, I've run the possible strategies and calculations through my head again and again: one mother; three kids; twenty-four hours in a day; movies to make; causes to support; interviews to attend; television appearances to make; a spacious home to keep clean and beautiful; and on and on. And then the truth becomes clear: one woman, however remarkable she is, even if she has the most amazing, supportive husband alive, could not accomplish all of these things without some serious help; let's face the facts: this woman has a staff!

I cannot know for sure the exact make-up of her staff because I don't know her personally, but I imagine, as I run through the possibilities, that she very likely has some combination of a personal chef, a housekeeper, a nanny, a personal shopper, an interior decorator, a laundry service, an accountant, a lawyer, a yard maintenance company, a travel agent, a makeup artist, a stylist, a personal trainer, a personal assistant, and that's probably just for starters. I don't begrudge her any of this support staff. I imagine she's earned every one of them. But, recognizing how much help she likely has at her disposal, I realize it's ridiculous to compare myself and what I can get done in my home and with my kids to a woman who very possibly has a staff of fourteen or so individuals just behind the scenes helping her do it all.

What about you? Could you use a break from the pressure you put on yourself to get it all done? If so, why not give yourself that break and try a kinder, more reasonable approach to getting things done (or not getting things done, as the case may be) as you navigate through your days? For starters, go ahead and throw out any comparisons you make between what you and other mothers seem able to get done in their lives. You don't know what their behind-the-scenes situations might be like—their financial means, the things they don't get done, the support and help they have that you might not have, the price they pay elsewhere in their lives to get so much done, and so on—so it's completely unfair to make comparisons.

Give yourself a gift and let go of those comparisons, and, as you do so, keep in mind that this is your life and you're in charge, so take charge. Don't let a lengthy to-do list, however carefully and enthusiastically constructed, be the primary dictator of the tone and pace of your days. Don't get me wrong, a to-do list has its place in motherhood and family life. But do yourself a favor and make sure you run the to-do list instead of letting the to-do list run you.

One of the simplest ways I know of to let my to-do list know who's boss is to set clear priorities about what absolutely must be done now and what I can live without getting done today or even tomorrow. To this end, I make full use of a standing daily to-do list that includes the must-do's such as the kitchen chores, feeding the pets, and our family's evening devotional (the kids, of course, participate in all three). To-do's such as these are absolutely essential to the smooth functioning of our home and family life. The other to-do list I make use of in my daily life is what I call my A-list or my hot list. It contains the things (such as scheduling a dental appointment or returning the library books) I need to get done, if at all possible, today, and if not today, tomorrow. These two lists together serve to relieve my stress and make things easier for me as a mom and a household manager.

I make use of two other to-do lists, although with much less emphasis than my standing to-do list and my hot list. There's my B-list, which has items I'd like to get done at some point but that don't have to be done right away. This list includes items such as painting the living room that new shade of moonlight or decluttering the garage. And then there's my C-list to-do's, like better organizing the bookshelves by subject category and condensing and editing my personal journals, which in reality may or may not ever get done.

There was a time when I felt that to be a competent home and family manager I had to get *everything* on *every* to-do list done, but I don't feel that way anymore. I want better for my children than a mother who exhausts herself with her perpetual race to the end of a never-ending to-do list. So now, in terms of getting things done, I allow myself to feel successful if I accomplish my standing daily to-do list and most of the items on my hot list. Anything I get done in addition to these two lists now feels like extra credit.

One of the best things about letting go of the need to be a mother who gets it all done is that I now have more time to focus on doing what matters most—just enjoying my children. They've never cared about whether I got it all done, but they do care enormously about the time I spend with them. I can recall a conversation I had with a friend a few years ago where we talked about the homes we grew up in. He grew up in a house that was always immaculate while I did not. I asked him if his mother had spent a great deal of her time cleaning house each day, and he responded, "That's what I remember most about my mom while I was growing up—her cleaning house." As we think about navigating our days and finding balance between doing and being, let's ask ourselves this question, "When my kids are grown up, what do I want them to remember about me and their time in our home?" When I think about the answer to this question, I think more often of putting down my to-do list than picking it up.

For the sake of your family and yourself, stop yourself when you begin to run yourself ragged, feeling as if you must get it all done today or tomorrow, and ask yourself another question, "Who says I must live this way?" And then, take a deep breath and review what you think you should be doing. Determine, based on your needs and the needs of your family, what you really must get done today, and what you can, with little worry, leave for another day. If you will give yourself the gift of paring down your to-do list to its bare essentials and leave some room for downtime and fun, you will discover firsthand this wonderful truth: there is indeed tremendous joy to be had in being a mother who doesn't do it all.

Invitations & Inspirations

- One of the best ways to turn a to-do list on its head is to drop everything and do something absolutely spontaneous with your children, perhaps an unplanned cookie baking session or a finger painting fest.

- Remember that no matter what you have accomplished or not accomplished today, if you have loved and nurtured your children, you have done what matters most.

- Most mothers have no real idea of how much they accomplish in a given day. Because, truth be told, much of what they do for their children and in their homes does not appear on their to-do lists. If you find yourself feeling discouraged about how much you think you're not getting done, take a day this week and write down everything you did with or for your family that day that wasn't on a to-do list. I suspect your head will spin with your accomplishments.

- Give your children and yourself a gift by putting at least one "just for fun" item on your to-do list every day. Make that two items—one to do with the kids and one to do by yourself or with your husband.

- On the days when I'm tempted to just barrel my way through the day, I recall the wise words of author Anne Morrow Lindbergh when she says, "Too many people, too many demands, too much to do; competent, busy, hurrying people—It just isn't living at all."[1]

❁ Imagine giving yourself and your family the gift of a day when you toss your to-do list out the window. What would you do with that day, and when could you make such a day a reality?

Notes

1 Maggio, ed., *The New Beacon Book of Quotations by Women*, 85.

It's Okay to Take a Nap

3

Becoming a well-rested mom can work wonders on your mood, outlook, and energy level.

I woke quite early one Monday morning—1:52 a.m. to be exact—to what sounded like a pony galloping down our stairs. This was alarming since we didn't have a pony, and, even if we did, we wouldn't let him into the house to gallop down the stairs, especially not at night.

Mumbling something about the galloping pony to my husband, I crawled out of bed to investigate the noise. Stumbling out of my bedroom, I turned the corner toward the stairs and there spied not a pony but a sweet little girl dressed in rainbow-striped shorts and a matching T-shirt, fully ready to greet the day.

She was not one of my children, but Rose, a friend's daughter, who was staying with us for several weeks that summer. On the previous Friday night, I had promised her

and the kids that I would take them to the doughnut shop first thing Saturday morning. However, they woke so late that morning that I told them we would need to wait until Monday morning to go and get the promised doughnuts. But, I advised them, if they really wanted to go and get doughnuts on Monday morning, they would have to wake much earlier than they had on Saturday morning.

Looking back, I realize now that I should have specified a waking time instead of letting the kids make any assumptions for themselves. I explained to Rose that while the doughnut shop was, in fact, open in the middle of the night (the drive-through, anyway), that it probably wasn't a good idea to wake everyone to head out for doughnuts just then. So I sent her trotting back up the stairs, hit the sack again myself, and woke six hours later to an entire herd of precious ponies galloping down the stairs.

This particular night was not the first time I had been awakened in the middle of the night by a child. There have been oh so many nights over the years when I have been up after midnight caring for sick little ones, comforting a child frightened by a bad dream, or providing a listening ear for a middle-schooler who's worried about a problem with a peer. My experience is not unique. Every mother I know faces a severe lack of sleep at times while raising her children.

For me, getting enough rest was not an issue in my pre-mothering days. If I wanted to sleep in on a Saturday or take a nap on a Sunday, who was to stop me? I confess

that I was wholly unprepared for the pervasive lack of sleep that comes with raising children.

Like most moms I know, I don't lose out on sleep due solely to the time I spend in hands-on caring for my children. Somewhere along the mothering path, I decided that giving up much-needed sleep was a reasonable way to get it all done, everything from keeping a tidy house to nurturing my burgeoning writing career. I was wrong. I don't handle sleep deprivation as well as I used to. In fact, these days, going short on sleep for anything more than a few days seems to be a sure recipe for a monster-mommy-meltdown.

The reality is that being short on sleep makes me far less than my best self. In other words, when I'm exhausted, I tend to be impatient, critical, and just generally grumpy with my kids. Not helping matters any is the fact that I sometimes experience a bit of anxiety with no clear cause. Research suggests that this anxiety may very well be caused by sleep deprivation. I've noticed that I'm especially anxious when I'm extra low on sleep. The same research shows that being chronically low on sleep can, in some cases, cause depression as well.

Also sobering are the studies that suggest that insufficient sleep may contribute to a person's weight problems. Carrying some extra pounds myself as I write this, I have to agree. I'm certainly more likely to indulge in sweets when I'm tired and looking for a quick, delicious pick-me-up than when I'm relaxed and well rested.

I can tell you from my own experience that becoming a well-rested mom can work wonders on your mood, outlook, and energy level. While I have yet to become an expert on getting enough sleep while raising children, I'm making great strides. For starters, I have come to believe that it's okay, and even highly beneficial, to take a nap whenever possible. There was a time when, as a mother, I was not completely comfortable with the idea of taking naps. I think I had the subconscious notion that they were a poor use of my time, that even if I had the opportunity to take a nap, I should do something more "productive" instead. I guess I felt deep down that naps were somehow unnecessarily self-indulgent. I was wrong about that. It's clear to me now that oftentimes what we moms need more than anything is a much-deserved nap to give us the energy and stamina we need to more fully meet our families' needs.

If you are ever in need of a nap and can possibly squeeze one in, by all means, do so. And do so without guilt. Keep in mind though that short naps, thirty minutes or less, are usually best because they take the edge off the fatigue without leaving you feeling groggy. Those short naps also don't usually make it difficult to fall asleep at bedtime.

As far as getting enough sleep at night, keep in mind that this won't happen unless you make it a high priority. If you're ready to make getting more sleep the priority it needs to be, consider what changes you might make in your life—perhaps leaving those cluttered kitchen counters until morning (keeping in mind that research shows we complete tasks more efficiently if we're well rested), letting your husband handle the bedtime routine with the kids, and turning off the late-night television (unwinding instead by reading for a few minutes before turning out the lights). If you need some motivation to get serious about getting more sleep at night, try this: imagine how good it would feel to wake up each morning feeling truly well rested, refreshed, and more than ready to take on a new day.

If you find yourself consistently tired and tired of being tired, consider giving yourself the gift of a "sleep camp." I'm not talking about going to a faraway place in the Poconos to get some sleep (although such a scenario certainly sounds intriguing). I'm talking about a sleep camp you can create for yourself by your own choices in your home. Make your sleep camp by giving yourself the gift of getting more sleep for the next twenty-one days. See for yourself what a difference such a sleep makeover can make for you and your children. To make this happen, consider putting your kids to bed earlier than usual so you can unwind and head off to sleep at a more reasonable hour yourself. Set a lights-out time for yourself, say, no later than ten o'clock. Keep in mind that getting everyone to bed an earlier hour will likely mean starting dinner and the evening routine a fair amount earlier than you're used to. It may take a few days or even weeks to adjust to an earlier schedule, but if you do what you can to make it happen, you and your family will reap enormous rewards.

I think most of us will agree that getting enough rest while raising children can indeed be a struggle, especially when we try to squeeze more activity into our days than is reasonably possible. Even so, I promise you that it is well worth the effort and self-discipline it takes to get more rest. After all, motherhood is so much more fun and enjoyable overall when we as moms are well rested, energized, and wide awake.

Suggestions for Dealing with Those Short-on-Sleep Nights

1. On the nights when a child is sick, make her a comfy bed with an air mattress and some blankets in your bedroom. Personally, I sleep better if an ill child sleeps in my room because I know I'll hear her and can be immediately available for her if she needs me.

2. If your spouse doesn't wake in the night as easily as you do to respond to a child's needs, lovingly wake him on occasion to take some turns tending to the kids.

3. I find that some soothing music played softly on the stereo can help mother or child return more easily to sleep. Consider listening to *Amarantine* by Enya or anything by Suzanne Ciani.

4. Try what we call a "warm cozy" at our house by purchasing or making a terry cloth–covered rice bag. When you're ready to use it, heat it in the microwave for a couple of minutes and then lay it on the abdomen of a restless child. This treatment is comforting and almost never fails to ease a child to sleep. This same treatment helps me relax and fall off to sleep on those nights when my mind doesn't want to slow down.

Invitations & Inspirations

- What would you be willing to give up to get more sleep—watching the late-night news, surfing the Internet, keeping a spic-and-span house, or _____ ?

- If you're still unconvinced that more sleep would be beneficial, or if you need some tips on getting some much-needed sleep, read one or more of these informative books: *The Promise of Sleep: A Pioneer in Sleep Medicine Explores the Vital Connection Between Health, Happiness, and a Good Night's Sleep* by William Dement; *A Woman's Guide to Sleep: Guaranteed Solutions for a Good Night's Rest* by Joyce Walsleben, PhD; or *The Well-Rested Woman: 60 Soothing Suggestions for Getting a Good Night's Sleep* by Janet Kinosian.

- If you think your taking a nap or getting eight hours of sleep at night in a comfortable bed is too self-indulgent, consider this: Louis XIV reportedly owned over four hundred beds and displayed a special liking for the especially spacious and luxurious variety. Give most moms the necessities of a dark room (or an eye-pillow), one bed, and some reasonable quiet, and she can usually take it from there.

- Give your children and yourself the gift of more sleep. Inda Schaenen, in her book *The 7 O'Clock Bedtime: Early to Bed, Early to Rise, Makes a Child Healthy, Playful, and Wise*, makes a compelling argument for getting kids to bed earlier in the evening. Even better, she tells you in detail how you can make it happen.

- Consider creating your own weekend slumber party (and I do mean slumber) by sending your kids to Grandma's house or leaving them home with Dad while you check into a hotel for some uninterrupted rest.
- What soothing bedtime ritual can you begin this week to help ease you into bed and off to sleep at a more reasonable hour?

A Laugh a Day Keeps Motherhood Fun

4

I agree that being a mom is serious business, but I think it's important that we as moms not take ourselves or our circumstances too seriously.

No one has ever accused me of being happy-go-lucky or even lighthearted for that matter. I think it's fair to say I take a fairly serious approach to life. I did so as a child and I do so now as a mother. This doesn't mean I never let loose and have a good laugh. I do, but sometimes I have to remind myself to relax a little and be open to the humor inherent in family life. Raising children is serious work, so, in some respects, I am very well-suited to the work of motherhood. Nevertheless, I have learned from firsthand experience that exercising a sense of humor and sharing a few good laughs with family members can benefit a mother tremendously, giving her a certain buoyancy, a sense of lightness necessary to creating a happy, and even joyful, home and family life.

Since I want, more than anything, to create a happy home and family life, I try to welcome humor and laughter into my home on a daily basis. When I'm feeling a tad too serious about my life and responsibilities and need some inspiration for lightening up, I rarely need to look any further than my own children. I find them to be a tremendous source of delight in the things they say and do. Every mother I know can recall some wonderfully funny or endearing things her children have said or done in the past, things that are sure to bring a smile to her face. Here are a few of the cute things my children have said over the years, things that, even now, can almost instantly lighten my mood.

"Mommy, I love that baby in your tummy. Who is it?"

My oldest daughter, now grown, said this when she was three years old and had just found out I was pregnant.

"This is so romantic!"

My second daughter, when she was three years old and having a tea party with her friend Grant. At thirteen, she's still very much the romantic.

"Mom, it's okay; I've been practicing."

My third daughter, when she was about three years old, and I found her climbing up rather high in a tree in our yard. This was her reassuring response when I pleaded with her to carefully climb down.

"Mom, the baby's going to be born with diapers on. I just know it!"

My fourth daughter, when she was three years old.

My daughters are not the only ones who tickle my funny bone. My four-year-old son has given our family some good laughs as well. One such laugh occurred on a Friday evening recently when our entire family was settled in the family room, everyone except me watching a movie. I was sitting at the computer trying to make headway on a writing project. About twenty minutes after the movie started, my son broke away from the screen and walked up to me, smiling, and reached out to put his arms around my neck. He then leaned toward my ear and whispered something that was clearly meant for just the two of us, "Mom . . . I love you the most!" He then gave me a hug and a kiss and went back to watching the movie with the rest of the family. I couldn't help but smile a little guiltily at hearing that I was my son's favorite.

A few minutes later, I looked up to see my son standing next to his dad, who was lying on the couch. He bent over his dad, whispered something into his ear that instantly brought a smile to my husband's face, gave him a hug and a kiss, and then returned to watching the movie. I couldn't help but ask my husband, "What did he say to you? What did he say?" My husband responded, almost sheepishly but smiling, "He said he loves me the most" to which I couldn't help but respond, "You too, huh?" We both laughed at the thought that he had said the same thing to both of us. But what was so precious and makes us smile even now is that we know our son meant it. He really loves each of us the most.

Over the years, I have learned firsthand that exercising a sense of humor can do wonders for a mom and family when it comes to dealing with the more challenging aspects of home and family life. For starters, my frustration level decreases dramatically when I look for the humor in a stressful situation.

For example, when I first became a mother, I couldn't for the life of me see anything funny about not getting enough sleep. I was taken so completely off guard by the sometimes astonishing lack of sleep that goes hand in hand with raising children that I was far more prone to complaining or crying about being so exhausted than laughing about it. Even so, in my years as a mother since then, I have enjoyed some unexpectedly good laughs due to a lack of sleep.

One such laugh came several weeks after the birth of my fourth daughter when my mind went fuzzy with fatigue. One particular night filled with nighttime feedings, I half-woke in a panic. I frantically searched through my purse for something I had lost. I woke my husband and said, "Barry, I've lost something. Will you help me find it?" He took my purse and began searching through the keys, checkbook, and stray papers. "What is it you lost?" he asked. "What am I looking for?" "The baby. I think the baby is in there." "Oh brother," he groaned and went back to sleep. I'm not sure how I came up with the odd idea that the baby might be in my purse, but I'm certain that a lack of sleep figured somewhere into the equation. All of these years later I can still recall that experience when I need a good laugh after a night short on sleep.

There have been many other times as well when I have benefited from tuning in to the more humorous aspects of the downsides of motherhood. I recall one period of time in particular when my children were very young and I found trying to get to the gym three times a week for a workout nothing less than a Herculean feat. There were, after all, children to sweet-talk into going to the gym, lost shoes to find and put on, and a toddler who absolutely detested riding in her car seat and so made the ride to the gym something to endure for all of us (we nicknamed her baby Houdini because she was so clever and persistent in her attempts to wiggle out of her car seat). I confess, the whole experience of getting to the gym tested my patience enormously. Nevertheless, I was determined to go because I knew I needed to workout if I was going to be the fit mom my children needed me to be.

So, in an attempt to see the humor in my seemingly humorless situation, I tried to imagine how an outsider might view my situation. And with very little effort I began to see, in my mind's eye, a comedy unfolding, something worthy of a big screen. Especially humorous were the scenes of a grown woman driving a van full of children to the gym while trying to keep everyone happy by singing, in rather animated fashion, a number of custom-designed verses of "Wheels on the Bus," including verses with cows, pigs, and hee-hawing donkeys having their say. To any outsider looking and listening in, we would have looked and sounded like a rootin', tootin' country bus specializing in farm-animal transport.

Not surprisingly, as I began to look for the humor in my attempts to get to the gym, the whole experience of getting to the gym became much easier. I believe this was the case because, as my mood lifted, my children's moods lifted and they cooperated with less effort on my part. A sense of humor can indeed be a mother's best friend.

This should be no surprise since research studies repeatedly show that laughter is especially good for us—whether that laughter comes from seeing a funny movie or recalling the funny things our children have said or done. I agree that being a mom is serious business, yet I think it's important that we as moms not take ourselves or our circumstances too seriously. In my opinion, few people need a good laugh on a daily basis more than a mom, so let's do ourselves and our children a favor and invite more humor and laughter into our homes and lives. As we do this, we will discover a wonderful truth—where we make room for laughter, we make even more room for love.

Invitations & Inspirations

- Take some time to recall and record the cute things your children have said over the years that bring a smile to your face. Such a record will be a tremendous gift for you and your children.

- Make a list of seven things you can do to invite more humor into your daily life. Act on your list and your whole family will lighten up and enjoy some good laughs.

- As the poet Langston Hughes said, "Like a welcome summer rain, humor may suddenly cleanse and cool the earth, the air and you."[1] What a gift a good laugh can be.

- Think of a frustration you have with motherhood and try to see it through the eyes of an outsider. Is there something, anything at all, that could possibly be funny about your situation if viewed through the eyes of someone on the outside looking in?

- More than one mother has told me that if something might be funny later, I should go ahead and let it be funny now.

- "Total absence of humor renders life impossible."[2] Let's not forget to allow ourselves at least one good laugh before the day is through.

A Few Good Books to Tickle a Mother's Funny Bone

Bete, Tim. *In the Beginning . . . There Were No Diapers.* Notre Dame, IN: Sorin Books, 2005.

Farmer, Debbie. *Don't Put Lipstick on the Cat!* St. George, UT: WindRiver Publishing, 2003.

Jones, Laura M. *Blow-Drying the Frog & Other Parenting Adventures.* Fairfax, VA: Family and Home Network, 2002.

Singer, Jen. *14 Hours 'Til Bedtime: A Stay-at-Home Mom's Life in 27 Funny Little Stories.* Deadwood, OR: Wyatt-Mackenzie Publishing, 2004.

Watts, Emily. *Being the Mom: 10 Coping Strategies I Learned by Accident Because I Had Children on Purpose.* Salt Lake City, UT: Bookcraft, 2002.

Five Movies to Make Your Family Smile

Yours, Mine and Ours (1968 version).

Cheaper by the Dozen (1950 version).

Anne of Green Gables (1986 version).

I Love Lucy—The Complete Series (179 episodes; 1951–57).

The Brady Bunch—The Complete Series (Seasons 1–5, 1969–74).

Notes

1. Deborah DeFord, ed., *Quotable Quotes: Wit and Wisdom for All Occasions from America's Most Popular Magazine* (Pleasantville, NY: Reader's Digest, 1997), 161.

2. Maggio, ed., *The New Beacon Book of Quotations by Women,* 331.

You Are a Queen, Not a Maid

5

I wasn't looking to make my children the household servants a queen would rule over, but rather, hoping to train them to become servants to themselves—doing their part to keep our kingdom reasonably tidy and in good order.

Has a child ever given you a gift that changed your view of yourself and your role in the world, or at least in your family? This happened to me several years ago when my then ten-year-old daughter gave me an unexpected present. Tickled to receive a gift for no apparent reason, I unwrapped the package and folded back the white tissue paper to discover a simple, sparkling white tile, about four inches square. On the tile, in black permanent marker, my daughter had printed these words, "My Mom is a Queen, Not a Maid. I love her." I looked up to see my daughter smiling at me and waiting for my response.

I was so surprised by her present that I hardly knew what to say. "Wow! Thanks. I love it," I told her as we shared a big hug. I had never received such a gift before and wondered how exactly she had come up with the idea for something so unique. I put the one-of-a-kind tile in a place of honor on my writing desk where I would see it often and be reminded of the sentiment it expressed.

My daughter's gift was certainly timely. She must have realized that I was well beyond my wit's end with her and her siblings, who had been frustratingly lax in doing their household chores in recent weeks. I was tired of repeatedly reminding my kids to clear the table and wash their dishes after dinner or to please put their dirty clothes in the hamper—yes, that's right, in the hamper, not on the bathroom floor or bunched up beneath their beds. My efforts had begun to feel like an exercise in futility, and I'm sure that I sounded more like a broken record than a mom when I chased my kids through the house calling out, "I am not your maid! I am your mother! Please pick up after yourselves!"

Given this recent history, I was surprised and delighted to receive a gift that suggested that my daughter had actually listened to me and apparently agreed that I was not the family maid after all. This was a happy day in my mothering life. I wondered, though, how she came up with the idea to proclaim in bold print that I am a queen. She never offered an explanation but left me to puzzle it out for myself instead. Although I didn't understand her reasons for calling me a queen, I confess that I rather liked this particular line of thought. Perhaps she was drawing on the fact that I was born in England; queens sometimes are. Or maybe she was thinking of our family genealogical history, which holds that we are descended from royalty, albeit royalty from a long, long time ago. These descendents, according to my bank account balance, are without any of the monetary advantages accorded to true royalty.

Whatever my daughter's reasons for writing that I am a queen, she had certainly given me something to think about. I hadn't felt like anything approaching royalty in a very long time. Instead, I had felt far more like a martyred peasant mother pathetically and unsuccessfully begging her children for help to clean the reigning queen's castle. Whose fault was this? Looking back, I have to admit that it was probably more mine than my kids'. After all, I agree with the experts who say that we parents teach our children how to treat us.

I wondered what would happen if I changed my approach to seeking help around the house. Would my kids change their behavior in response? Maybe if I acted more queen-like in my expectations of getting their help they would be more compliant in giving the help that was expected of them. I hoped so. I wasn't looking to make my children the household servants a queen would rule over but rather hoping to train them to become servants to themselves—doing their part to keep our kingdom reasonably tidy and in good order.

So where to begin? A queen would have started by issuing an official decree, so I created my very own "Decree of Family Chores." I brainstormed a list of household chores that the kids could help with, divided them up, made a plan to rotate the jobs through the kids, and typed up a very official looking, decree listing the household chores.

Looking back, it might have been fun if I had delivered the decree on ancient-looking scrolls. Maybe I'll do that yet. Even so, writing the household chores down on paper, in black and white, so no one can dispute who has to do what job on which day works far better than me having to re-create the chore wheel every day. This more organized approach has decreased frustration levels for everyone in our family, especially me.

While issuing a decree assigning household chores has been useful in managing our family kingdom, it alone is not enough to get things done. I've had to take a look at how I express my expectations for getting my kids to help around the house. I realize now that running through our house exclaiming, "I am not your maid! I am your mother!" has probably done little to persuade my kids to help. A queen, in seeking assistance in her kingdom, shares her expectations with dignity, with an air of authority, with self-respect, expecting to be fully respected by those she leads. Sounds good in theory. I'm working on behaving more queen-like in practice. As a result, my kids are taking me more seriously now when it comes to doing their part to keep our castle clean.

I've discovered, though, that the real secret to getting help around the house is to establish consequences for those who don't do their part. Queens, over the centuries, have certainly understood the importance of consequences—"How dare you defy my decree! If you continue to defy my orders, it will be off to the dungeon with you!" While the dungeon threat may work for queens, I don't generally recommend that it be used by moms. In my case, I've found that different consequences work for different kids. With my oldest daughter, who is now fourteen, I can often be heard to say, "Remember, you can't talk on the phone until your chores are done." My younger kids know that they must complete their chores before they watch TV or invite a friend over. I admit that I'm still working at being consistent in enforcing these consequences, but thankfully I'm making progress.

I tell my children that living in a reasonably tidy house can make us all feel a bit more like royalty. I also tell them that since I'm the queen of our household, they get to be the prince and princesses. I remind them that as royalty we will conduct ourselves with dignity and self-respect whether we're sitting down to a feast fit for a royal family or sorting through the laundry and scouring the bathrooms. I will always appreciate my daughter's gift as a reminder that we moms do not have to be the maids. If we're willing to change our perspective and do the work necessary to train our kids, we can rightfully be the queens that we truly are.

Invitations & Inspirations

⚙ Debbie Bowen's book, *W.O.R.K. (Wonderful Opportunities for Raising Responsible Kids)*, provides a down-to-earth and wonderfully instructional and inspirational guide for helping us teach our children how to do their part to help our homes run smoothly.

❧ Create your own inspiring sign to put on the refrigerator, reminding you and your children that you are indeed a queen and not a maid.

❧ I promise you that if you will spend time teaching your kids how to clean house now, you will reap great rewards, and sooner than you might imagine. Remember, your job is to work your way out of a job by teaching your kids to do their part. That's the only way they will be ready to head out on their own someday.

❧ Find easy ways to keep the house clean together. Here are two strategies that work well in our home:

1. Have "tidy-up times" right before every meal, but especially just before supper.

2. When the state of the house starts getting on your nerves, get a laundry basket or two, put some energizing music on the stereo, set the timer to seven minutes, and invite your children to run around the house with you picking up everything that's out of place and putting it into the basket to put away. You'll be amazed at the difference you and your children can make in just seven minutes.

❧ If you are short on time or too tired to get your house in the shape you'd like, try the "piece of heaven" advice my friend Celeste shared with me years ago. Choose one room in the house and tidy it up (with the kids' help, of course) until it feels like a piece of heaven. Forget the other rooms for now and just enjoy your little piece of heaven. When you're feeling up to it, this room will inspire you as you tackle other parts of the house too.

⚙ Always keep Phyllis Diller's advice in your back pocket; you never know when it might come in handy: "If your house is really a mess and a stranger comes to the door, greet him with, 'Who could have done this? We have no enemies.' "[1]

Notes

1 Maggio, ed., *The New Beacon Book of Quotations by Women*, 325.

Motherhood Is Full of Wonderful Surprises

6

I began to make conscious efforts to open my mind to the possibility that my life as a mother was far more wonderful, just as it was, than I had previously realized.

As I was walking through the wooded greenbelt in our neighborhood with my husband, our three-year-old son, and our Australian Shepherd, I felt a sudden rush of joy and the immense sense that I live a wonderful life. I know this sounds terribly gushy, but please hear me out. I haven't always felt so content. There was a time when I was rather prone to bouts of self-pity in my role as a mother.

During that time, I tended to focus on the downsides of motherhood—the lack of sleep, the almost nonexistent time to myself, the ever-present needs of my children, the never-ending cycles of laundry and housekeeping, and the overall disparity between my romantic notions of parenthood and the realities of raising children.

Not helping matters any were a surprising number of the magazine articles I read during that period of time that focused primarily on the downsides of motherhood—article after article written by moms disillusioned with the arduous process of raising kids. Looking back, I realize now that those types of magazine articles, with their negative slants, probably did much more to sell the advertiser's products than articles that invited mothers to focus on and feel good about their experiences in childrearing.

I was fairly well stuck in an overall negative mind-set about my life when I happened across the philosophy of Sonia Choquette, an author and life coach, that struck me with its implications on motherhood. She said she believed that we see what we're looking for in our lives and we create what we focus our attention on (to some, this may sound obvious, but in regards to motherhood, it hadn't been so for me until then).

Taking this powerful kernel of truth, I began to make conscious efforts to open my mind to the possibility that my life as a mother was far more wonderful than I had previously realized. My first step in seeking a shift in perspective was to begin keeping the much-touted gratitude journal, and I will tell you that by engaging in that one activity alone, I felt a shift in my mood. As I wrote item after item, I was thankful for in my role as a mother. Day after day, I was amazed to realize just how much I had to be grateful for—my children's health, their senses of humor even at young ages, their smiles just when I needed them, and so much more.

Taking time to write down what I was grateful for as a mother made me more observant of the positive in my life. As I went through my days, I became more and more aware of the good as it happened.

Another experience helped me immensely during this period as well. A friend shared with me how much she absolutely loved being a mother. She said that while being a mother was a surprising amount of work and that, overall, raising children was far from a perfect experience, she found immense joy in the perfect moments that abound in sharing a life with children. That was it. She had captured in words what I had known and felt in my heart but had not until then fully realized—motherhood is not perfect, but, oh, there are so many perfect moments to enjoy with our children if we are awake to them.

With my friend's words of wisdom came a much-needed shift in my perspective. I let go of my unrealistic expectations of motherhood overall and became more aware of those perfect moments and embraced them as they occurred. And there are so many perfect moments every day—the early morning sleepy-head hugs, the little hands tucked in mine, the unexpectedly warm conversations shared with my teen, the impromptu family games of kickball, and so many others. As I recorded my blessings in my journal and became alert to the wonderful, unblemished moments of joy, my overall satisfaction as a mother grew.

Yes, my efforts at being more positive about motherhood were, for a time, especially conscious, but now looking for the good and focusing on the positive in my mothering life has become second nature for me. And I now see clearly the truth about motherhood I hadn't seen before—that it is the experience I make of it. And so I choose, through what I focus on, to make it absolutely wonderful.

Five Wonderful and Unexpected Surprises I Have Experienced in Motherhood So Far:

1. A sense of wonder can be contagious. Children are innately curious about the world around them, and if we spend any time at all with them without rushing, we will be reminded ourselves of just how amazing this world is. There's the butterfly in the garden just outside the front door, the tempting rainy-day puddle on the sidewalk, and the friends waiting to be made at the neighborhood park, just to name a few.

2. If you carry hurts from your own childhood, they can be healed, in part, by giving your children what your parents could not give you.

3. The world does not end when you step out of your comfort zone. Watching my thirteen-year-old daughter, who is terrified of being in the spotlight, sing a solo in the school choir and play a violin solo in her orches- performance inspires me to develop and share my nts even when I'm nervous about how others might nd.

up with a newborn infant in the middle of the at times, more wonderful than most might After all, the household is quiet, the lights are turned down, and it's just the baby and me without interruption, getting to know one another.

5. Following our children's interests can lead us to our own. My children play the piano, flute, and violin, and they sing in church and school choirs. Other than a half-hearted attempt at piano lessons, music didn't play much of a part in my childhood. Inspired by my children, I plan to take piano lessons again myself.

Invitations & Inspirations

❀ A wise man by the name of Walt Streightiff once said, "There are no seven wonders of the world in the eyes of a child. There are seven million."[1] Anyone who's spent any time at all with children can't help but agree.

❀ Consider reading *Mitten Strings for God: Reflections for Mothers in a Hurry* by Katrina Kenison. Her book provides pure inspiration for embracing the wondrous potential of motherhood and family life.

❀ What are some of the unexpected and wonderful surprises you have discovered so far about being a mom? Start a small journal to capture some of those surprises for you but also for your children so they will have a written record of just how much you loved being their mom.

❀ Tell your children now how much you love being their mom. Share with them some of your discoveries about motherhood as they happen: "Wow, I never thought I would go roller skating again, but thanks to you, I gave it a try and I had fun!"

❁ Ask your mothering friends how they have been surprised by joy in motherhood. Their answers will touch and inspire you in your own journey through motherhood.

❁ I agree wholeheartedly with author Marni Jackson's exclamation that "motherhood is like Albania—you can't trust the descriptions in the books, you have to go there."[2] Motherhood is, in so many ways, far more amazing than anything I could have imagined before having kids myself.

Notes

1 DeFord, ed., *Quotable Quotes*, 57.
2 Maggio, ed., *The New Beacon Book of Quotations by Women*, 459.

You Deserve a Break Today

7

As mothers, our methods for finding time off may differ, but the results are usually the same—happier moms and thus happier families.

I remember well the afternoon several years ago when I couldn't help but count the minutes until my husband was due home from work. It had been a tough day with the kids, and as much as I loved them, I was ready for a break. When my husband walked in through the front door, I attempted to put on a good face—the one that says, "Welcome home and I hope your day has been as pleasant as ours." Instead, the grumpy, exhausted me let my dear husband have it when I surprised even myself by blurting out, "I'm going on vacation . . . I'll be back in fifteen minutes." I offered no explanations, just passed the baby off and headed to our bedroom, where I shut the door and leaned against the wall, sliding down into a crumpled heap on the floor.

What next? I wondered. I wasn't sure, since I hadn't planned on taking this vacation. It was a short vacation, to be sure, but even so I was struggling to figure out how to spend the fifteen minutes I had so spontaneously seized. The problem was that I was out of practice. After all, I couldn't recall the last time I had taken a real time-out. Motherhood doesn't have to mean being on duty 24/7 day after day, week after week, but I had allowed it to become just that, and now in my burned-out state, I realized that such an approach to motherhood isn't necessarily good for my kids or for me. Sitting there doing nothing, I could feel the time ticking away, but I didn't care. This was my vacation, wasn't it? I could spend it however I wanted.

Just when I was sure I wouldn't come up with a fully satisfying way to spend the remaining few minutes of my time-out, I remembered my former yoga instructor's wise counsel. She had advised her students to take a time-out, however short, every day to focus on the simple act of breathing in and breathing out without rushing and without becoming distracted by those never-ending but always demanding to-do lists. So I lay down on my back, closed my eyes, and breathed in and out, in and out, relaxing more and more with each succeeding breath. When my fifteen-minute retreat time ended, I walked out of the bedroom to rejoin my family. I felt noticeably refreshed and surprisingly ready to navigate through the busy evening ahead. We still had dinner to eat, soccer practices to attend, unfinished homework to complete, and bedtime routines to drive through, but I was sure now that I could do it.

I found myself wondering why I hadn't acted on my former yoga instructor's advice more often. I could have saved myself more than a few bouts of burnout. While I couldn't fully answer this question at that moment, I had the nagging notion that I was at least partly to blame for my sometimes frazzled state. After all, I remembered the time when my husband, listening to me once again express my need for some time off, had exclaimed, "I can't give you what you won't give yourself!" Somewhere deep inside, I think I believed that "real moms" don't take time off. How can you be a real mom if you selfishly take focused, uninterrupted time off to care for yourself when you could be doing something, anything, for your kids? Sounds a bit martyr-like, don't you think? Such thinking, I now realize, was hurting more than helping my family and me. I needed to find a more graceful, less anxious way to move through motherhood.

I'm glad to report that, in recent years, I have found some satisfying and realistic ways to fit nourishing downtime into my mothering life. Ideally, I like to begin and end my days gently. I used to go full throttle until late in the evening, whether I was cleaning house, working on a project for church or my kids' school, or discussing family finances with my husband. Often, I crawled into bed so late that once my head hit the pillow, I was immediately out cold. Inevitably, the next morning I couldn't peel myself out of bed until I absolutely had to for the sake of my kids. This vicious cycle repeated itself again and again until I discovered the benefits of bookending my days with quiet.

Overall, my days seem to go more smoothly when I wake thirty minutes or so before my kids begin to stir. When I get up early, I generally take a quick shower and then spend twenty minutes or so in quiet solitude—either writing in my journal or nourishing myself spiritually through scripture study. Sometimes I may even go for an early morning walk.

These sessions of solitude truly influence the quality of life for my entire family. When I emerge from my early morning quiet time just as my children are waking, they are quick to catch my calm yet enthusiastic mood. This positive atmosphere seems to wrap us all in a wonderful sense of anticipation for the day ahead.

At day's end, I've learned the importance of winding down before my head hits the pillow. Taking the time to read something enjoyable, to reflect on what went well that particular day, and to say a prayer before I go to sleep soothes my spirit and makes for a more relaxing rest, and thus a less anxious, more enjoyable tomorrow. Sometimes, when I'm in need of some extra time off in the evening, I ask my husband to manage the bedtime routine alone. Beginning and ending my days as softly and slowly as possible serves as a spirit-energizer in the midst of motherhood. I'm a better mother when I take these necessary time-outs.

Over the last few years, I have also tried to give myself and my kids the gift of quiet time in the middle of the day when we're home together. After lunch, the nappers go down for sleep while the non-nappers are encouraged to do something restful, or at least quiet. This gives me a chance to take a quick nap myself, read a book, or do some writing in the middle of the day. It gives my non-nappers the opportunity to learn how to be by themselves, or at least to play quietly with a sibling. While I'm sometimes tempted to use this midday time to catch up on housework, I generally resist the urge to do so because I benefit so much more from those midday mini vacations. They do much to refuel my body and spirit in preparation for the afternoon and evening ahead.

Making a conscious effort to bookend my days and striving to have some downtime after lunch seems to work well for me. Even so, every mom I know has to discover for herself what works best for her and her family when it comes to necessary downtime. My older sister does well by taking one evening off a week while her husband takes care of their children. She enjoys planning how she will spend her evening away from home and always comes back feeling enormously refreshed. My younger sister likes to take her baby on long walks in his stroller. They both come home feeling refreshed and content. Many of my mothering friends find great success in trading childcare with another mother, giving each other a break. As mothers, our methods for finding time off may differ, but the results are usually the same—happier moms and thus happier families.

Wouldn't it would be nice if we could count 100 percent on having time off every day for a little self-renewal? But this isn't always realistic. After all, things come up— kids get sick, spouses travel, and some days are simply full, from beginning to end, with necessary have-to's. The good news is that if you've consistently taken necessary time for self-care in recent weeks, you'll likely do fine without any downtime for a few days. You'll have some reserves to draw upon. If, however, time has been marching on and you find yourself feeling especially depleted and burned out, perhaps you should ask yourself one simple question, "When was the last time I took some time off?" And if the answer turns out to be "I can't quite remember," perhaps it's time to begin making some plans. Because the truth is, you deserve a break today, and no one is going to give it to you if you will not give it to yourself.

Invitations & Inspirations

❀ The prolific author Alexandra Stoddard was right when she said, "A time set apart each day, when you can unwind, be in touch with and restore yourself, is as necessary as a nutritious diet and enough sleep."[1]

❀ How does taking regular downtime make a positive difference for you as a mother? Write your answers on a slip of paper and tape them to your bathroom mirror to motivate you to take needed time off.

❀ Consider reading *Gift from the Sea* by Anne Morrow Lindbergh, the wife of Charles Lindbergh. Her classic and eloquent book describes honestly and hopefully the perennial struggle women face in meeting the needs of their families while taking care of themselves.

⚙ Make a list of five 15-minute retreats you could create to renew yourself when time permits. How about a journal-writing session, an extended prayer, or maybe simply crawling into bed and relaxing for a few minutes?

⚙ Consider purchasing and using *The Stretch Deck* by Olivia H. Miller. It's a boxed deck of fifty 5x7 cards, each illustrating easy-to-follow stretches. Try just three or four stretches in one session and you'll feel surprisingly renewed.

⚙ If it is impossible to break away from your children to have some much-needed time to yourself, invite them to share some downtime with you. Light a candle, put some soothing music on, and share some stretching time together. My preschooler loves choosing which stretches we'll do from *The Stretch Deck*.

Notes

1 Alexandra Stoddard, *Living a Beautiful Life* (New York, New York: Avon Books 1986), 90.

You Are an Amazing Mom

8

When we take the time to note the good in ourselves, we feel better about ourselves, so we can better see and respond to the positive in our children.

I am blessed to have some terrific mothering friends. They are wonderful friends to me and amazing mothers to their children. There's my friend Becky, who struggles with chronic illness and yet raises her three children with enthusiasm and gusto. There's Victoria, a native of Sweden, who's raising her three children in the United States with her American husband and doing everything she can to steep her children in the beauties of both cultures and languages. And then, of course, there's Nancy, a mother of twelve who never ceases to astonish me with her commitment to meeting the individual needs of her children, not letting any one of them get lost in the mix. As wonderful as these mothers are, I wonder if they know for themselves just how amazing they are as the mothers to their children.

In my experience, few mothers know how truly terrific they are. Instead, many moms, myself included at times, tend to focus on what we're not doing well, on how we don't compare to the mother next door and how, just maybe, we'll never become the good (translation: perfect) moms we think we should be.

Because so many mothers I know tend to dwell on their mistakes, weaknesses, and failures while overlooking much of the good they do, I can't help but ask, "What's the payoff?" How are we as mothers served by being so hard on ourselves? Focusing on our imperfections keeps us humble to be sure, but few moms need more humility than they currently possess.

While I believe there is value in identifying what's not working and what we think we should be doing better, I think most moms could benefit from taking some time to note the good they're already doing. In the workplace, positive feedback comes in the form of performance evaluations received from your supervisor. In motherhood, we serve as our own bosses, and if we're going to be anything approaching fair bosses to ourselves, we would do well to give ourselves a break and acknowledge the good we are doing as the mothers to our children.

Could you benefit from taking a kinder view of yourself as a mother? I know there was a time earlier on in my mothering experience when I was sorely in need of giving myself a break in how I viewed myself as a mom. If you find yourself in similar shoes, try giving yourself the gift of acknowledging the good you're doing as a mom now.

If possible, take time today, right now or perhaps just before bedtime tonight, to make a list of twenty or so of the things you have done well in the past or are doing well now in your mothering life. Note specific instances recently where you have felt particularly good about your work as a mother, such as, "Today, I stopped cleaning house to spend focused time playing checkers with my son." And be sure to include things you are doing consistently well over time—"I read to my children each night and sing them a lullaby before tucking them into bed and whispering good night."

Continue to build your list of the good you have done until it includes at least twenty items. If you find you can create a longer list, by all means, keep going. There are bound to be days when you will need reminders that you are doing well overall as a mother.

Once you have finished creating your list, consider making it a habit to carve out a few minutes every day to write something in your journal that you did well as a mother on that particular day. And yes, you can write more than one thing if you want to. In fact, I recommend it.

If you will take these steps—creating a start-up list of the good you have done as a mom and then noting in a journal the good you do each day—you will likely find an increased lightness and joy in your days. You will still see what you want or need to improve upon in your work as a mother, but I predict you'll no longer feel defeated by an unfair focus on the negative. Rather, you'll be uplifted and energized by recognizing and honoring the good you do. This has certainly been the case for me over the years as I have gone from being unnecessarily hard on myself as a mom to acknowledging the good I see in myself.

I promise you that if you will focus on the good you are doing as a mother, you will discover for yourself some important truths—namely, that you do not have to be a perfect mom to be a good mom, and that you are a better mother than you sometimes think you are. In fact, you'll likely see, whether you realize it now or not, that in many ways you are a truly amazing mom. Keep in mind, though, that it is one thing for me to tell you these truths, but it will be quite another for you to discover them for yourself. Will you accept my invitation to become more aware of the good you are doing now as the mother to your children? If you accept this invitation, you will be giving yourself and your children a precious gift.

After all, as mothers, we want our children to see themselves as capable in their lives. And what better way to ensure this end than to be a mother who feels capable and conveys confidence in herself. When we take the time to note the good in ourselves, we feel better about ourselves and so we will better see and respond to the positive in our children. Remember, we cannot give our children what we do not ourselves possess. If we want to nurture confidence within our children, we must first nurture it within ourselves.

Invitations & Inspirations

⚬ For one week, imagine seeing yourself through the eyes of a close and caring friend who only knows how to look for the good in you. One week off from being unnecessarily hard on yourself might be one of the best gifts you could ever give yourself and your children.

⚬ Husbands and children, as wonderful as they are, are not generally given to lavishing appreciation on the wives and mothers in their lives. Why not write yourself a letter of appreciation for all the good you do as a mom. You could begin as follows, "I think you're doing a terrific job as a mom . . ."

⚬ Give other mothers the gift of looking for the good they're doing and let them know, in very specific ways, what you see. I must tell you that I have found an extra special kind of joy when I have noticed another mother doing something well—perhaps taking the time to lovingly brush and braid her daughter's hair or kneeling on the floor to look into her child's eyes when she talks to him—and made a point of telling her the good I see. Her smile in response never fails to remind me of how much a mother wants to make a difference in her world and how wonderful it is to hear someone say that she does.

⚬ For one full day, seek to think and say only kind things about yourself. If this is an easy thing to do, terrific. But if it's not so easy, work to make it a habit. You'll be glad you did.

⚙ The truly happy moms in the world are almost invariably the moms who recognize the good in themselves. Remember, you are an amazing mom in many ways whether you realize it or not.

You Really Can Complete Thoughts While Raising Kids

9

For me, mothering is a meditation. It has taught me to focus, not necessarily on what I had originally intended to do, but rather on what needs to be done most at this moment.

Scene One: I'm in the kitchen making my family's favorite chocolate cake. My four-month-old is sitting in her stroller beside me. I finish mixing the cake and take one last look at the recipe to make sure I have included everything. Enter nine-year-old daughter. "Mom, can I please have a friend over? Oh, please, *please* can she eat dinner with us? I haven't had anyone over since yesterday!" Listen to daughter, plan response, anticipate reaction, smile at now fussy baby, and pop cake into oven. Mission accomplished. Five minutes later, pull cake out of oven and attempt somewhat successfully to stir in forgotten baking soda.

Scene Two: Squeeze in an errand on the way to five-year-old's soccer practice—all my kids in tow. Take a different route to the ball field. Not sure which freeway turn-off to use coming from this direction. Radio is turned up a bit loud to satisfy budding adolescent's tastes. My nine-year-old daughter loves music, but even more, she loves talking loudly over loud music. Continue driving through rush-hour traffic, noise buzzing in the background. Lose focus. Miss turn. Become frustrated and arrive fifteen minutes late for soccer practice.

Scene Three: Goal is to put sharp scissors into the cupboard above the microwave and checkbook back into my purse. Begin. Pick up checkbook while holding baby and listening to five-year-old say, "Aren't we going to be late for the doctor's office? Huh? Huh? Mom, aren't you listening to me?" Become distracted. Lose focus. Think goal is met. Start walking out the door with my kids. Discover checkbook is missing. "Why isn't my checkbook in my purse? I just put it in there." Turn to three-year-old who has been getting into everything lately. See three-year-old but no checkbook. See scissors still sitting on counter. Look above microwave. Checkbook found.

I'd like to say that these scenarios are isolated incidents, that they happen, say once a month or maybe even once a week; but the truth is, they happen more often than my kids take baths. Much more often. Mothering does this to me. These are just three of the many cases of Constant Interruptus that I have experienced over the years. I used to get really frustrated at how impossible it seemed to have a complete thought while raising my five precious inter-rupters, but not anymore. I love my kids and plan to raise them to adulthood, so over time I have developed some sanity-saving coping skills.

First, I have given myself permission to put my children on hold occasionally. I don't know where I developed the belief that I have to be fully present every minute of every day, hanging on their every word. Perhaps it's the cumulative effect of all the parenting books I have digested over the years telling me that I don't want to damage their self-esteem by not paying adequate attention. The truth is, my children will have a rude awakening if they grow up expecting others to pay complete attention to them whenever demanded. So doing myself and my children a favor, I sometimes tell them, "Hold on, I'm doing something right now that needs my full focus. Keep that thought and I will listen to you in a moment." They learn some patience while I drive safely through traffic, successfully complete a cake, or finish a phone call.

As the family manager, I sometimes forget important information (like a phone number or a rescheduled music lesson), because I didn't write it down as soon as I received it. I used to think that I would remember the date and time for so-and-so's follow-up dental appointment and didn't need to write it down. But between the dentist's office and home, I may have had five or six separate conversations with one or more of my children and can no longer remember anything except the most recent conversation. So, write it down. That's my motto.

Often I find that as soon as I commit myself to fixing dinner or paying bills, I can count on one of my kids wanting or needing my attention. This used to leave me feeling frustrated and discouraged about completing a job before I even started. But over time I've learned that I don't necessarily have to stop what I'm doing to give a child the attention she needs. Sometimes my kids simply want to be a part of what I'm doing, so I'll invite them to share in completing the task, perhaps by measuring flour or stamping envelopes. Together, we finish the work and create some good memories.

Like most mothers, my days are full of activity from start to finish. I become forgetful, frazzled, and mistake-prone when I have had too little downtime to collect my thoughts and rest my spirit. For me, solitude-time is essential to maintaining balance and perspective. I used to feel guilty about taking time out for myself, but I traded in the guilt for the conviction that happy kids are raised by happy moms. A little time alone does a lot to make me happy. I agree with Anne Morrow Lindbergh when she says, "It is a difficult lesson to learn today—to leave one's friends and family and deliberately practice the art of solitude for an hour or a day or a week. . . . And yet, once it is done, I find there is a quality to being alone that is incredibly precious. Life rushes back into the void, richer, more vivid, fuller than before."[1] I don't have a day or a week for solitude, but I have been changed by finding an hour.

Over time, I have accepted that interruptions are often just a natural part of family life and are best taken in stride. More times than I care to count I have been heading out the door with just enough time to make it to an appointment when I discovered that the freshly diapered baby needed to be changed again. Becoming frustrated only made things worse. Instead, I have learned to lighten up, to surrender to the inevitable interruptions, finding that it makes much more sense to arrive late and happy than late and grumpy.

On a recent hectic, interruption-filled day, I read an article about a nun who lives in an adobe hut in the New Mexico desert—alone. It sounded inviting. I wondered if she would mind a roommate. There was a time when I could have chosen a more solitary life where I would have had innumerable hours to collect my thoughts, to complete a given task—but I didn't. I chose marriage and motherhood.

Over the years I have learned that mothering is a meditation. It teaches us to focus, not necessarily on what we had originally intended to do, but rather on what needs to be done most at the moment. Sometimes we need to navigate safely through traffic or make dinner, putting our interrupters on temporary hold. But many other times, we need to stop what we're doing and accept a child's interruptions as an invitation to slow down, to savor the small but meaningful moments that add up to a rich family life.

Invitations & Inspirations

⚙ *Busy but Balanced: Practical and Inspirational Ways to Create a Calmer, Closer Family* by Mimi Doe provides wonderful support for navigating motherhood with sanity and grace.

❀ Ask your mothering friends how they deal with the start-and-stop nature of raising children and managing a household. They will likely share some humorous stories but some wise counsel as well.

❀ Brainstorm a list of solutions for getting things done, such as the laundry, meal preparations, and so forth while caring for your kids. You may be surprised by just how many solutions you can come up with for getting necessary things done while also tending to your children.

❀ When you find yourself getting too caught up in those ever-present to-do lists, consider these wise words from Sophocles: "Children are the anchors that hold a mother to life."[2]

❀ Another wonderful sentiment to help a mother keep perspective when faced with those inevitable interruptions is this one expressed by Evelyn Nown: "Perhaps parents would enjoy their children more if they stopped to realize that the film of childhood can never be run through for a second showing."[3]

❀ De-stress by finding a way to carve out an hour a day to tackle your to-do list without interruption. Perhaps you could find that time while the kids are watching a movie or your husband is reading to them. On the other hand, find ways to carve out time to have a daily "Children's Hour" when you tune out the to-do lists and other household distractions (like the ringing telephone) to share quality time with your children.

Notes

1. Anne Morrow Lindbergh, *Gift from the Sea* (New York: Pantheon Books, 1975), 42.
2. DeFord, ed., *Quotable Quotes*, 56.
3. Ibid.

Exercise Will Energize Your Family Life

10

As mothers, we cannot afford to only pay lip service to our self-care.
We and our children deserve better.

Imagine a mother who, on a daily basis, radiates warmth and energy, conveys contentment, and seems clearly anchored in calm. Imagine meeting her and asking her to reveal her secret formula for maternal happiness. You find she's more than willing to share, so you quickly tuck away your rising envy in anticipation of hearing some dramatic and expensive revelation, something to the effect of her having a personal chef and a housekeeper who handle the daily have-to's while she spends uninterrupted fun time with her kids. No, it's nothing like that, you discover. Rather, it's something far more stunning in its simplicity. Her secret, she confides, is contained in two words and two words only—exceptional self-care.

You look at her in disbelief and ask, "Really, that's it?

That's all it takes? Taking good care of yourself really makes that much of a difference?" Looking directly into your eyes, she readily affirms, "It makes *all* the difference."

While I haven't experienced a conversation exactly like this one, it captures well the essence of some of the eye-opening conversations I have shared with the truly happy moms I know. More often than not, the moms I know who seem genuinely content make taking exceptional care of themselves a top priority. They do what they can to get enough sleep and take solitude time for mental, emotional, and spiritual renewal (see chapters three and seven for encouragement in these areas). But they also make it a priority to fuel their bodies with nourishing, well-balanced diets and to energize themselves with regular exercise. This self-care, they claim, makes all the difference in how they feel as moms, and, not surprisingly, it has a positive impact on how they nurture and care for their kids.

Early on in my mothering life, I made taking good care of myself a high priority, especially during the period when I was going through a divorce from my first husband and adjusting to life as a single mother to my toddler. During that time, I exercised whenever I could and, in the process, made some wonderful memories with my daughter. We spent a lot of time together exploring the trails around our city's lake. I walked or jogged while pushing my daughter in her stroller as she took in the sights and chattered away to me and anyone else who would listen. I recognized at that time that taking good care of my body was essential, not only to my physical health, but to my overall sense of well-being as well. So at that time I was absolutely committed to getting the exercise I needed. And, to be honest, I took it for granted that I would continue to take good care of myself as I raised my daughter and any other future children I might someday have. I was wrong to do so.

By the time I remarried and gave birth to two more children, I had stopped taking such good care of myself. Of course, I had the best of intentions to start exercising tomorrow, always tomorrow, but rarely did I realize them. Deep down, I felt I didn't have the time to work out anymore. And, I rationalized, I didn't really need to work out. After all, wasn't being a mom, with all the physical activity involved in caring for little ones, exercise enough? As it turns out, it wasn't even close.

After the birth of my third daughter, I started having back problems. And after the birth of my fourth daughter, my back problems worsened, leaving me debilitated at times to the point where I could barely get out of bed some days. Not only was I having back problems, but I was more exhausted physically than I had ever been in my life. And while I agree that fatigue does, to some extent, go hand in hand with mothering young children, I wasn't sure that I needed to be quite so tired in my quest to be a good mom.

When I visited the family doctor with my complaints, wise and compassionate man that he was, he wasted no time in telling me that my problem was quite simple: it was me. My abdominals had become weak. I was more tired and stressed than necessary because I wasn't taking good enough care of myself, and I wasn't getting the exercise my body needed. He told me that as physically demanding as raising children can be, I needed to start taking much better care of myself if I wanted to be fully up to the task of raising them.

Heeding my doctor's counsel, I made a plan to start getting more regular exercise right away, rather than tomorrow or someday down the road. As part of that plan, I joined a gym where I could walk or jog on the treadmill and lift weights. Interestingly, once I worked myself back into shape, which didn't take as long as I thought it might, my back problems diminished. In fact, now that I think about it, I haven't been bothered by severe back problems of any sort in more than seven years. And I find that over-all I am a much more content and energetic mom than I was when I wasn't exercising. Clearly, the doctor was right. By not exercising, I had made my life as a mother more work and less fun than it had to be.

So in the last seven years or so, I have consistently made working out a top priority. I can assure you it hasn't been easy. One thing I've learned for sure about being a fit mom is that if you're going to be a mom who exercises any-thing approaching regularly, you're going to have to be a mom who is flexible about how and when she exercises. My commitment to working out is firm, but my workout plan is fluid, changing in response to the needs of my family. These days, I typically jog for thirty minutes each weekday through my neighborhood or a local park and then go to the YMCA three times a week to lift weights. And while this exercise routine is my plan A, I tap a variety of backup plans from B to Z for exercising, including jogging on the treadmill or swimming at the Y, riding bicycles with my children, working out to an aerobics DVD with my kids, and taking a late evening walk with my husband.

If necessary, I can be very creative about how I get my exercise. For example, several times in the last year I have resorted to jogging inside my home because I wanted desperately to run but a bad ice storm made it unsafe to even step outside my door. My family tells me I look quite the sight when I jog through the living room, the kitchen, the family room, up the stairs, down the hall and back down the stairs again, only to repeat the circuit some twenty times or so before I stop. I have learned from experience that the right way to get exercise while raising kids is simply to get exercise whenever and however you can.

When I'm extra low on motivation, I simply remind myself that I always feel better after I work out. And working out literally makes me a better mother to my children. After all, when I get regular exercise, I have more energy overall, more patience, and more fun being a mom. What mother doesn't want to have more energy, patience, and fun with her children?

As mothers, we cannot afford to only pay lip service to our self-care. We and our children deserve better. If you haven't made self-nurturance a priority in your life, start now. If you will do this, you will experience a notable difference in your daily round—perhaps an energetic calm long absent from your life or more joy and spontaneity in the time you spend with your children. After a week or so of practicing the self-care basics, you'll discover that exceptional self-care doesn't necessarily involve a nanny or a full-time cook. Rather, exceptional self-care more reasonably involves performing the basics of self-care consistently over time and, because you have the energy to do so, throwing in a comforting treat here and there, whether it's taking time to read the novel that's beckoning from your nightstand or making time to take a candlelit bubble bath.

If you have any doubts about taking time to take care of yourself through exercise and other means, be assured that taking good care of yourself is an excellent way of taking care of your children. Accept the invitation to be a mother who takes good care of herself through eating healthfully, exercising, and so on and you will become a mother who blesses her children's lives with energy and calm—a mother who, through her example, beckons other mothers to a more joyful path.

Invitations & Inspirations

- ⚬ What price have you paid for not taking better care of yourself? Has it been worth it? Do you want to continue paying that price? If not, what are you willing to do differently, starting today?

- ⚬ For inspiration in self-care, read Alice Domar's *Self Nurture: Learning to Care for Yourself As Effectively As You Care for Everyone Else.* In her book, Domar, the director of the Mind/Body Center for Women's

Health at Harvard Medical School, shares specific meditation and relaxation exercises as well as essays encouraging and supporting women in their self-care.

⚙ Brainstorm a list of at least ten different ways you can get exercise while raising children. Here are two ideas to get you started. Why not wake up forty minutes before the kids to jog on a mini trampoline while listening to an audio book on your mp3 player? Or turn on some energetic music and dance around the family room with the kids—spinning, jumping, leaping, and reaching for the sky. Your list will serve as a powerful reminder that it is possible to get and stay fit while raising children.

⚙ Keep in mind that if you will exercise and make a point of staying fit, you are more likely to raise kids who will exercise and stay fit.

⚙ If you haven't been exercising regularly, set a goal to exercise five or six days a week for the next three weeks. Before you begin, use a page or so in your journal to write down how you are feeling mentally and physically, and then at the end of three weeks revisit that page and write about how you are feeling now. I suspect you'll see a surprisingly positive difference.

⚙ I appreciate Edward Stanley's reminder that "those who think they have not time for bodily exercise will sooner or later have to find time for illness." Moms must, for the sake of their children and themselves, make time for exercise.

Your Love Matters More than You Know

11

It seems clear to me that the secret to a mother's love is not that it be perfect in its delivery but rather that it be showered in abundance over her children's lives.

When I walk into my bedroom these days, I experience an extra sense of delight because posted above my bed is a ten-foot-wide banner with the words, "Welcome Home, Mom!" emblazoned in a rainbow of colors. Equally vibrant pictures and love notes surround these words, all drawn and written by my children, to welcome me home after a recent and unexpected trip out of town. As I read my children's messages, "You're the best, Mom!" and "I love you; I missed you!" and take in their carefully rendered drawings of family life—including our home; our cat, Oliver; and various family members—I can't help but feel loved. And even better, I can't help but recognize that my children feel loved too. Truth be told, my children's welcome home banner, so thoughtfully created, serves as a wonderful affirmation of my work as a mother. I am reassured by the clear evidence it provides that my love matters to my children, that my love and care make an important and notable difference in their day-to-day lives.

Every mother has experienced similar moments—moments when she has felt truly affirmed in her work as a mother, times when she has felt, unequivocally, that her love matters. Perhaps these moments have occurred for you when your baby smiled and giggled as he looked into your eyes, or when your preschooler made her way through a crowd of people to throw her arms around your neck and exclaim, "Mommy, I love you so much!" or when your teen, despite a sometimes cantankerous attitude, presented you with a Mother's Day card clearly selected or created with just you in mind. Such affirming moments can be a wonderful gift, not only for us but for our children as well, if we are fully alert to recognizing and responding to them. What mother doesn't want to know that the work she does as a parent matters? And what child doesn't benefit from having a mother who feels affirmed in her work as their mother?

In my experience, soaking up and savoring these affirming moments can make for some precious shared memories and a closer connection with our children overall. They can also, I have discovered for myself, provide a positive counterbalance to those times when a child's message, either through their words or their behavior or both, seems to be, "I don't like you. I don't want you around!" Any mother who's been at the work of raising children for more than a year or so has very likely experienced just such moments. As moms, we strive to be a pretty thick-skinned and tough lot, but those moments of seeming rejection can sometimes still hurt even the toughest of us.

I find it helpful to keep in mind that sometimes our children need our love and care the most when they seem to want it the least. This has certainly been the case with each of my five children. I remember one time in particular when my youngest and oldest child (two and fourteen years old at the time) both chose to express their intense displeasure with me at the exact same moment. This memorable occasion happened one weekday evening after a busy day filled with school and after-school activities. My husband was out of town on business, and I was attempting to bathe my two-year-old son. My son was letting me know, in no uncertain terms, that he was in no mood to take a bath when in walked my fourteen-year-old daughter to inform me for what seemed like the umpteenth time that she must, absolutely must, have her own cell phone and no later than the very next day. Her situation appeared, if you didn't know the whole story, to be nothing less than a matter of life and death.

I will not soon forget that stressful evening—me leaning over the bathtub trying to bathe my two-year-old who was kicking, splashing, and screaming, "I don't wanna take a baff! I don't wanna take a baff," while my teenage daughter called out behind me, "Mom, I need a cell phone. I've got to have a cell phone. I'm the only kid in my school who doesn't have a cell phone! Please, Mom, please! You have to get me one! Can we get it tonight?" Although this situation was stressful, I couldn't help but laugh a little on the inside, realizing that I could never have imagined myself in such a scenario before I had children.

The easy thing to do that night would have been to end the bath early and let my daughter have the desperately desired cell phone. But the loving thing to do, despite my children's protests, was to stand firm on the bath and the cell phone. After all, my son needed a bath to stay clean and healthy and my daughter didn't "need" to have a cell phone at that time and didn't yet have the maturity and self-restraint to manage her cell phone usage.

My children didn't fully get it then that my choosing to stand firm with them was more loving, not less, than if I had let them have their way. Although I was frustrated with their behavior, I wasn't so frustrated with their feelings and lack of understanding because, frankly, I know there were times while I was growing up that my mom didn't let me have my way. And looking back, I realize now just how much she loved me to put up with my protests and tell me no anyway.

When I stop to think about it, I realize that it wasn't until I became a mother myself that I understood just how much my mother loved me and in how many ways she showed her love on a daily basis that I didn't fully recognize at the time. Looking back, my mother's love impacted my life far more than I realized while I was growing up and far more than I think she could possibly have known herself.

Now, as I mother my own children, I look back and stand in awe of all the ways my mother loved me that I can only begin to appreciate now. There were the times when she cared for me in the middle of the night when I was sick and feeling pitiful (I understand now that she was very likely terribly exhausted herself on those nights, but I would never have known from the way she cared for me); the times when she transported me from activity to activity as I stayed busy with sports and other school activities, as well as the times when she listened to my teenage woes over my relationships with my friends or boyfriend. She wove her love into my life so naturally, so completely, that I had no real awareness of the time, love, and effort she must have expended in my behalf on a daily basis.

Just as I didn't fully understand how much my mother's love mattered in my life while I was growing up, our children cannot possibly fully understand how very much we love them and how so much of what we do in our daily lives is because of our love for them. Even so, we wake up every morning and love our children with our words, our caring, and our actions. Being a mom, I have found, is an invitation to love more fully through hands-on care and service than I ever imagined loving anyone before I had children. Most of us, I believe, are not even fully aware ourselves of just how much love we pour into our children on a given day—there's the physical care (providing meals, clothes, baths, hugs and kisses, and so on) as well as the emotional, spiritual, and intellectual care (the listening ear, the counsel shared, the stories read, the homework help). Loving our children can be completely exhausting and yet entirely exhilarating in the same day.

For all this talk about a mother's love, I think it's safe to say that a mother's love is, more often than not, far more complex than most Mother's Day cards would suggest. There is certainly, in the case of the mothers I know, a mother-love that is warm, tender, and compassionate—a love that runs deep and constant—just like those cards suggest. But the truth is, real mother-love dispensed by real mothers is earthier, less perfect than the lofty ideal espoused around Mother's Day. And that is just as it should be—real love, in all its imperfections and glory, for real children. Let's not waste our time striving to give our children a seemingly perfect Stepford wife–like mother-love—all sugar and honey but somehow lacking in depth—when they (and we) are far more likely to thrive and experience genuine joy when we give them a passionate mother who loves them imperfectly (yes, she has been known to lose her cool at times) but loves them well.

With all of this said, it seems clear to me that the secret to a mother's love is not that it be perfect in its delivery but rather that it is showered in abundance over her children's lives. So keep doing what you're doing—loving your children in the best way you know how, day in and day out, and know that as you seek to shower your children with your unique brand of love on the days they accept it and on the days they seem to reject it, you will be giving them what they need most to grow and thrive in your home and in the larger world. And just in case you ever lose sight of the impact of your love on your children's lives, be assured that your love matters far more than you can possibly know.

Invitations & Inspirations

- As author Alexandra Stoddard said, "Mothers, across cultures, are at the emotional center of the home, and collectively, of the world. They are channels of loving energy, the primary nurturers of all human beings."[1] Being a mother is indeed an enormous responsibility, but it may also be, I believe, the recipe for living a truly joyful and meaningful life.

- Consider the love you received or didn't receive from your mother while you were growing up, and use your childhood experiences to become more conscious of making choices about the kind of mother-love you want to nourish your children with as you raise them.

- I couldn't agree more with author Debbie Bowen when she says, "As mothers, we occupy a unique and cherished spot in the hearts of our children. We must not underestimate the power of our position."[2]

- What are your strengths in showering your children with mother-love? Hugs and kisses? A listening ear? Reading animatedly to your children each night before tucking them in? Celebrate and make the most of your particular strengths and you and your children will be blessed.

- It's never too late to say thanks. If you feel moved to do so, take time to write your mother (or the mother figure in your life) a letter to say thanks and to let her know what you appreciate about how she cared for you and the things she did then and now that have made a positive difference in your life. Moms love knowing that their love matters even after their children are grown.

❁ If you are aware of children who do not have a mother in their life, or whose mother is somehow not able to give them the love they need, reach out to those children. Every child yearns to be mothered because, after all, there is nothing like a mother's love. And each of us can help fill in the gaps.

Notes

1. Alexandra Stoddard, *Mothers: A Celebration* (New York: William Morrow and Company, 1996), xi.
2. Debbie Bowen, *Nobody's Better than You, Mom* (Springville, UT: Cedar Fort, 2007), 4.

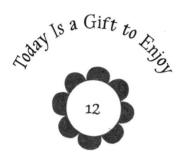

Today Is a Gift to Enjoy

12

We cannot know for sure what tomorrow will bring to our homes and families, but we can become more conscious of fully embracing and enjoying the gift of today with those we love.

Late one July, just a day after we returned home from a wonderfully relaxing and enjoyable family vacation, my husband and I were hit head-on with some wholly unexpected and potentially devastating news. Earlier that morning, I had gone to an appointment for what was sure to be an uneventful ultrasound to confirm my doctor's theory that I had a small, non-cancerous tumor in my lower abdomen. That same evening, only hours after the ultrasound appointment, the phone rang. It was my doctor calling to tell me that she needed to refer me for a surgical evaluation right away. According to the ultrasound report, the mass was larger than expected—the size of a large grapefruit—and looked suspicious. In effect, based on the results of the ultrasound, it was possible that I had ovarian cancer, and, if I did, it was likely advanced and the prognosis would not be good.

I was absolutely blindsided by my doctor's phone call. *Cancer? Me? A mother of five young children who almost never slows down for anything, potentially facing a fight for her life with a cancer that is notorious for being relentless?* I couldn't fathom the possibility. Sure, I had been tired in recent months and a bit sluggish overall, but cancer? The days that followed were, in some respects, a complete blur, but in other respects they were lit with a clarity and fire I had not previously experienced in my life. I have always been what my friends and family call a truth-seeker, one who strives to live at the heart of life, not wasting time on what's not important and focusing my attention on what I feel truly is important. But this cancer scare, a scare that came out of nowhere, made it clear, in ways my life had not previously, just what was important and what was not.

Not for a moment during those worrisome days did I regret that I had never returned to my birthplace in England (a long and passionately held desire) or that I had not published more articles and books or that I had not kept a tidier home. In fact, I didn't get locked into regrets at all. They were a waste of time, it seemed to me, and if I had cancer as advanced as the ultrasound suggested was possible, I did not want to waste any time at all.

What I did want to do was spend as much focused, quality time as possible with my children and my husband.

Spending such time with them had always been important to me, but sometimes such time got lost in the never-
ending priority shuffle inherent in modern life. Regardless
of my ultimate prognosis, I did not want to let another
day slip by without making as many meaningful connections and memories as possible with my children and
husband.

Despite the sense of urgency I felt about spending
more quality time with my family, my husband and I
made the decision not to bring life as our children knew it
to a sudden halt. Instead, we determined to work around
our children's usual activities—school, of course, but also
music lessons, soccer practices and games, and church
activities among them—to make more concentrated time
as a family. Overall, it was easy to stay the course with these
activities because our children loved them and thrived on
them. These activities served as powerful and reassuring
anchors during a period of uncertainty. So rather than
overhauling every aspect of our lives, my husband and I
chose instead to step up our commitment to the rituals and
activities we already shared with our children that helped
us to create and maintain our sense of family. We did this
realizing that each day is a gift and that we as parents have
a responsibility to make the most of the gift of each day
with our children.

Here are a few of the simple but meaningful methods we established to make the most of each day with our
children.

Morning Prayer

There are few things that set the tone for our days as individuals and as families more than how we begin our days. I try to awaken each morning before my children get up so I can have some time to myself. Once my husband and I are both up and in gear, we wake our children and invite everyone down to the family room for family prayer. We kneel together around our round coffee table and one person—a different person each day—offers a prayer of thanksgiving and asks that a spirit of peace and love be present in our home and family that day. This single shared activity as a family at the beginning of the day serves as an almost sure-fire recipe for making the most of that day. When we begin our mornings with such a reverence for the new day, each member of our family seems more naturally attuned and able to make the most of the day for themselves and with others.

Hellos and Good-byes

In all the hustle and bustle of family life it can be so easy for family members to leave the house and return home without sharing any real good-byes or hellos. Early on in our married life, my husband and I made it a point to take unrushed time to say good-bye or hello when either of us left the house or returned home each day. We have continued this tradition with our children and have made it a very important part of how we stay connected as a family.

Somehow over the years our good-byes with our children have evolved into a not-to-be-missed "hug, kiss, and nose-rub" ritual they can't bear to go without when mom or dad leaves the house. When my husband or I announce that we're leaving the house to go somewhere—whether to go to work, to run an errand, or whatever the case may be—the kids come running while calling out, "Hug, kiss, nose-rub, hug, kiss, nose-rub!" and we stop long enough to share just that with them—a hug, a kiss, and an Eskimo-inspired nose rub before we walk out the door. It seems to me that everyone in our household feels deeply loved from this one ritual alone. After all, who doesn't want to be valued enough to warrant a special greeting or farewell when they come or leave home?

Evening Devotionals

Evening devotionals are the most recent addition to our recipe for staying connected and making the most of each day as a family. We began our devotionals as an attempt to meet our family's need for some shared spiritual nourishment and as a way of staying up on what's going on in each other's lives. As it turns out, our evening devotionals have become much more than either of those two things alone. We usually start our devotionals around eight o'clock, and they rarely last longer than fifteen to twenty minutes. Believe it or not (and my kids couldn't believe it when I first suggested this idea), when we come together for devotional, we start by singing a favorite hymn. We then share a scripture or other meaningful spiritual reading. These two activities bring an immediate spirit of peace and reverence into our home. Each member of our family has a night of the week to be in charge of picking the hymn we sing and the scripture we share and discuss. We all look forward to our turn.

After our singing and scripture time, we invite each family member to tell about something positive they experienced or accomplished that day, big or small. We often clap for one another at the announcement of good news and have even been known to share standing ovations when they seem called for. We have created many wonderful memories as we have kept this nightly tradition of sharing good news. There have been times when a child has announced a good grade they made on a tough test, a kind act of service they performed for someone at home or school, or a goal they achieved to clean out their closet or to master a certain song on the piano. I always look forward to sharing good writing news with my children and husband when I have met a writing goal and completed a newspaper article or written a new chapter in a book I've been struggling to write. Sometimes my children cheer so wildly for my writing accomplishments you'd think I'd won the Pulitzer Prize.

After all the exciting announcements are made and the applause and cheers die down, we talk about the next day's activities—who needs to be where, how we can each support each other, and so on. And then, just as we did at the beginning of the day, we come together around our coffee table to offer a prayer of thanks and to ask for a good night's rest and guidance in the day to come. Ending our day in such a peaceful way paves the way for a good night's sleep and energy and enthusiasm for another day to come.

As we have sought to be consistent in maintaining these and other comforting and connecting rituals as a family, we have grown notably closer and made memories of days not to be forgotten.

I am grateful to report that, despite a terrible scare, I am cancer free. A skillful surgeon removed the suspicious-looking mass, which turned out to be a rare form of ovarian cancer. Thankfully, in my case, the cancer was completely contained within the tumor itself, and, although I will be under watch for the rest of my life, my health prognosis is excellent. Even so, my heart goes out to the moms who, even as I write this, are fighting in one way or another for their lives. They know the truth that the rest of us some-times lose sight of—today is truly precious, more precious than we sometimes realize. Today is a gift for us as mothers to share with our children in the most loving ways pos-sible, a gift that we can, with less effort than we might sometimes realize, make the most of with our children.

Making the most of today doesn't have to mean making elaborate plans and spending hours in preparation. Rather, it means focusing on the small but meaningful ways we as parents can show our children love such as sharing hugs often, looking into our child's eyes when we speak with him or her, and letting them know with our words, tones, and actions that we love and value them.

We cannot know for sure what tomorrow will bring to our homes and families, but we can become more conscious of fully embracing and enjoying the gift of today with those we love. If we will slow down to more fully enjoy the gift of today with our families, we will come to know firsthand what too few individuals know—that having children and being a mom can make life sweet in ways others cannot possibly imagine.

Invitations & Inspirations

∘⚙ Think of one family ritual you would like to begin or renew, perhaps a Friday night game night or a nightly storytime before tucking the little ones into bed. Keep your ritual simple and do it regularly and your family will thrive on the increased connectedness, the joy of sharing your days together.

∘⚙ When the days begin to blur with the speed of too much busyness and you find you haven't spent enough time together as a family, announce a Drop-Everything-and-Do-Something-Fun-as-a-Family activity. We usually do these on Saturdays, and either my husband or I will announce the activity early in the day, "At three o'clock we're going to drop everything and go swimming" or "At six o'clock tonight we're going to unplug the phone, grill burgers, and play board games."

∘⚙ Shared spiritual nourishment is essential for creating a sense of family and inviting a sense of peace to reside in our homes. How would you like to better nourish your family spiritually? A morning walk through the greenbelt or a spiritual reading just before dinner? Brainstorm the possibilities and experiment to determine what works best for you and your family.

✿ To the extent possible, share a sit-down meal together every day. This can be an especially challenging thing to do as your children grow older and become more and more involved in their own activities. Even so, share meals with your children, or substitute a family bedtime snack on those truly hectic days, and you will reap the reward of closer family connections.

✿ Begin each morning with this simple question, "What gift do I want to give my children today?" and you will create some wonderful days in response.

✿ Before today comes to an end, gather your family together and give thanks for all that is good in your life. Giving thanks will most assuredly multiply the pleasure you and your family take in the gift of today.

Be Kind to Yourself—You Won't Regret It

13

Now that I think about it, it is a real curiosity to me that we as moms are not more easily kind to ourselves. After all, it makes sense to be kind to the person who provides so much care for our children.

Most of us can get away with being hard on ourselves for a time, whether being hard on ourselves means not getting enough sleep or exercise, taking ourselves too seriously, or whatever the case may be. Even so, there are times in our lives when circumstances demand, whether we're in the habit or not, that we be kind to ourselves.

One such time in my life occurred during the days, weeks, and months following my cancer surgery. I was so elated by the good news we received the week after the surgery that I thought surely I would be back up to speed in no time at all.

Even so, I learned the hard way that recovery from major surgery takes time, more time than a full-throttle mother like me is interested in giving. During the first few weeks after the surgery, I had no choice but to rest. If I started to do something even a bit too ambitious, I would find myself almost immediately overwhelmed with fatigue, so much so that I could do nothing but crawl into bed, pull the covers over my head, and succumb to sleep.

But then a few weeks into recovery, when I felt more myself, I determined to get more done. My doctor had counseled me to be sensible, to listen to my body, and to heed its messages. I realize now that if you're going to hear what your body has to tell you, you have to slow down long enough to hear and process the messages it has to share.

I will never forget the morning following a day of doing too much when I awoke at 5 a.m. in an astonishing amount of pain in my lower back and left leg. Unfortunately, my husband was out of town. I could barely get out of bed but somehow managed to drag myself up the stairs to tell my seventeen-year-old daughter that something was wrong with me and I wasn't sure whether to be worried or not. In my lower back, left hip, and down through my left leg and toes, I felt an odd mixture of pain, including a burning sensation, feelings of compression as if someone had wrapped my leg too tight in a bandage, as well as a pins and needles sensation and persistent numbness. My daughter attempted to rub my back some and to comfort me with her words of reassurance. After a few minutes of her tender care, I made my way downstairs to take some pain medication. I tried to shake it off and go back to sleep but couldn't.

Around 7 a.m., I called a friend who was a doctor

and was himself all too familiar with back problems. He asked me about my activities of the previous day to which I sheepishly responded with the fact that I had been on my hands and knees scrubbing a friend's floor (helping her to prepare for a move), cleaning out my children's closets, and . . . well, he got the picture. He shook his head and gave me firm instructions for some much-needed self-care, the most important one, he said, being that I get some rest and try not to do too much.

I'd like to say that I heeded his every word and that the back problems disappeared overnight. But things didn't work out that way. Looking back, it was almost entirely my own fault. During the next couple of weeks, every time I felt just a bit better, I would attempt to resume normal activities. I remember telling my husband that I wanted to hurry up and get better. He responded, in the most loving way possible, that "the notion of wanting to hurry up and get better is your biggest problem."

Even now, as I look back on that time, I'm surprised by how determined I was to "hurry up and get better." I realize now that my tough-girl approach caused setback after setback, the worst being when I was at my sister's house for Thanksgiving and because I was so determined to participate in meal preparations and other activities despite my tenuous health, I did too much and set my back into such spasms that I became incapacitated and useless to anyone during that holiday visit.

At that point, I was so humbled by my physical circumstances that when my husband asked me, "What do you think you're supposed to learn from this experience?" I responded, finally getting it, that "I need to be kinder to myself." And clearly the kind thing to do at that time was to stop hurrying up to get better so I could give my body the time and space it actually needed to heal once and for all.

I will not forget that lesson, and although I wouldn't wish that experience on any mom, I would wish for every mom to have the same sense I finally got of how important it is that we as moms be kind to ourselves. Certainly it is true in the physical realm of taking care of our bodies, but it is also true in the realm of nourishing and caring for our minds and spirits as well.

Now that I think about it, it is a real curiosity to me that we as moms are not more easily kind to ourselves. After all, it makes sense to be kind to the person who provides so much care for our children.

And so I wrote this book for you and for me as a reminder that we as moms must be kind to ourselves. It is essential for our well-being as well as for the well-being of our children. Just in case there's any confusion, let me be clear that being kind to yourself is not a selfish act, not in the sense that we as Americans think of selfishness. Truly, it is not. Author Elizabeth Gilbert, in a television interview with Oprah Winfrey, said that we Americans would do well to reconsider our definition of selfishness. She says that in Mandarin Chinese there are two words for selfish. One means to do something that is beneficial to yourself and the other means to do something that is greedy, hoarding, or cruel.

Few mothers I know are greedy, hoarding, or cruel. Many mothers I know would do well to do things that are beneficial to themselves and therefore beneficial to their children. So consider being kinder to yourself in some of the ways I mentioned earlier in this book—by taking a nap when needed, by recognizing that you are a better mother than you sometimes think you are, by giving yourself a break when it comes to trying to get it all done today. And while you're at it, consider some other ways you can be kinder to yourself as well. Maybe it's time to forgive yourself for the mistakes you've made as a mom; we all make them and our children generally survive and even thrive despite them. Or consider developing a stronger support network with your mothering friends; there's nothing like feeling part of a village when raising your children. Maybe the kindest thing you can do for yourself is to set aside some real time for you and your spouse to enjoy being together as a couple without your children, as precious as they are.

Whatever the case may be, will you develop the habit of being kinder to yourself than you have been in the past? Keep in mind though that making the commitment to being kinder to yourself doesn't automatically make it easy to carry out. In my case, taking good care of myself following my surgery required a surprising amount of patience and self-discipline. Among other things, I had to learn to say no when I really wanted, but was not in a position, to say yes; I had to take time for gentle walks and lots of stretching; and I had to surrender, in some respects, to a messier house than I liked to keep. But being kinder to myself paid off in a big way as persistent self-kindness was the only path back to my formerly healthy self.

If you have any doubts about what difference self-kindness can make to you and your family, give it a try. Start small. Consider some of the ways you can be kinder to yourself today and make the commitment to do so until you go to bed tonight. Then tomorrow, make the commitment to be kinder to yourself again, and the day after, until the weeks, months, and years add up.

Of all the truths I have shared in this book, I hope you will remember this one: It's okay to be kind to yourself. In fact, I highly recommend it. If you choose kindness when it comes to how you treat yourself, I promise you will not regret it. Because the truth is, if you choose to be kind to yourself day in and day out, you and your family will most assuredly be blessed. For you will be a mom who knows a valuable secret to creating a happy home and family life.

Invitations & Inspirations

✿ Consider the times in your life when you have neglected to be kind to yourself. What were the consequences? Was it worth it? Resolve to be kinder to yourself in the future.

✿ Here are a few additional suggestions for being kind to yourself: give up the guilt that hurts more than helps; ask for help when you could use some; buy yourself an inexpensive gift such as a book. *Furry Logic: A Guide to Life's Little Challenges* by author and illustrator Jane Seabrook is sure to bring a smile to your face.

- Do something kind for another mother. Deliver a surprise dinner. Drop off a box of chocolates and a note of admiration for the good she does. Offer to babysit so she can go for a long walk or browse through a bookstore.

- Create a kindness jar. Take small colorful slips of paper (use a rainbow of colors) and list one simple kind thing you can do for yourself on each slip of paper. Then fold the slips of paper, put them into a clear canning jar, and set it on your fridge. When you are in need of some self-kindness, pull out one slip of paper for inspiration.

- Remember, if you are kind to yourself, you will give other moms permission to be kind to themselves as well.

- As the author Amelia Barr reminds us, "Kindness is always fashionable."[1] Let us make it so in how we treat ourselves.

Notes

1 Maggio, ed., *The New Beacon Book of Quotations by Women*, 375.

About the Author

DEBRA SANSING WOODS is a full-time mom and part-time freelance writer. Her writing often focuses on and celebrates home and family life. Her articles have appeared in numerous publications, including *LDS Living*, *Meridian* magazine, two Deseret Book anthologies (as a contributing author), the *Dallas Morning News*, the *Athens Review*, and others. She is also the author of *Mothering with Spiritual Power: Book of Mormon Inspirations for Raising a Righteous Family*.

Debra graduated from the University of Texas at Austin with a BBA in accounting and went on to become a CPA and corporate controller. She also taught as a highly rated instructor of personal finance for the University of Texas Informal Classes. She currently lives in Oklahoma City with her husband, Barry, and their five youngest children. Debra's family also includes her husband's three grown daughters.